BEST FOOT F

West Sussex

David Weller

COUNTRYSIDE BOOKS

NEWBURY BERKSHIRE

First published 2011
© David Weller 2011

COUNTRYSIDE BOOKS
3 Catherine Road
Newbury, Berkshire

To view our complete range of books,
please visit us at
www.countrysidebooks.co.uk

ISBN 978 1 84674 228 6

Maps and photographs by the author

Designed by Peter Davies, Nautilus Design
Produced through MRM Associates Ltd., Reading
Typeset by CJWT Solutions, St Helens
Printed in India

Contents

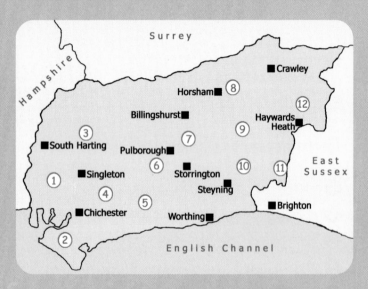

■ Area map showing location of the walks ■

Introduction

What a great joy it is to explore the glorious West Sussex countryside. I generally use a leisurely speed because I am more likely to be rewarded with sightings of wildlife close up; perhaps deer grazing at the forest edge, a hawk soaring overhead or baby rabbits frolicking in a meadow. A slower pace also allows for the discovery of interesting wild flowers, or fungi and lichen that could easily be missed otherwise.

Another pleasure is to investigate the history and architecture of a pretty village en route, or to call in at the local pub and enjoy the hospitality at a table in a sunny garden. Many routes are ideal for picnicking, so why not pack a sandwich and a drink and enjoy lunch alfresco amidst beautiful scenery?

The walks are in the glorious South Downs, Britain's newest National Park, so it is inevitable that some of the circuits involve a hill or two but they should not trouble anyone of average fitness; just take your time and enjoy the fantastic scenery. I have also included a place of interest close to each route which you may wish to visit to complete your day.

I recommend that you wear walking boots as they offer grip in mud and support on uneven ground. My maps are drawn to scale and have numbers that correspond to each paragraph of the text, but for a better overview of the circuits I have listed the relevant Ordnance Survey Explorer map at the beginning of each walk.

So, enjoy these leisurely walks and remember; the longer you take the more of interest you will see!

Publisher's Note

We hope that you obtain considerable enjoyment from this book; great care has been taken in its preparation. Although at the time of publication all routes followed public rights of way or permitted paths, diversion orders can be made and permissions withdrawn.

We cannot, of course, be held responsible for such diversion orders and any inaccuracies in the text which result from these or any other changes to the routes nor any damage which might result from walkers trespassing on private property. We are anxious though that all details covering the walks are kept up to date and would therefore welcome information from readers which would be relevant to future editions.

The simple sketch maps that accompany the walks in this book are based on notes made by the author whilst checking out the routes on the ground. They are designed to show you how to reach the start, to point out the main features of the overall circuit and they contain a progression of numbers that relate to the paragraphs of the text.

However, for the benefit of a proper map, we do recommend that you purchase the relevant Ordnance Survey sheet covering your walk. The Ordnance Survey maps are widely available, especially through booksellers and local newsagents.

1

Stoughton Down and the Monarch's Way

■ *The wonderful vista from Stoughton Down* ■

This tranquil and beautiful walk begins by following a track through magnificent indigenous woodland that is home to a good deal of wildlife, including deer. Without too much effort, the route gains 200 ft in height and reaches its turning point where a wide track offers easy walking through the forest and brings you to the open expanse of Stoughton Down where the views are quite breathtaking. The way descends from these heights along the Monarch's Way long-distance path to reach the hamlet of Stoughton from where it begins its return on a woodland path lined by wild flowers during the summer months.

Distance: 4½ miles

Starting point: Stoughton Down car park. GR SU815125

How to get there: Stoughton Down is 5 miles north-west of Chichester. Half a mile west of Chilgrove on the B2141, go west on a lane signed to East Marden and pass south through the village to reach the car park after ¾ mile.

OS Map: Explorer 120 Chichester

Refreshments: Picnic along the route or visit the Hare and Hounds pub in Stoughton (tel. 02392 631433).

The Walk

1 With your back to the road, leave the left side of the car park on a gravel track alongside woodland. Forty yards after woodland encroaches on your left, fork left on a signed grassy bridleway. Now keep ahead at all times, later passing an isolated house.

2 At the top of a rise lined by yew trees, turn right on a forestry track signed as a bridleway. After ¾ mile, continue alongside the fence of remote **Blackbush House** and keep ahead passing a five-bar gate. After 140 yards, turn right on the signed **Monarch's Way** and follow a wide track to reach the edge of woodland.

At 615 miles, the Monarch's Way is the second longest of England's long-distance paths. Using public rights of way and bridleways, it follows as closely as possible the route taken by King

■ *Admiring a line of beech trees near the start of the walk* ■

Charles II to evade capture after his defeat at the Battle of Worcester in 1651.

3 Ignore a crossing track and press on along the bridleway where wonderful panoramic views over Stoughton Down open up. Remain on this marvellous path, passing farm buildings, until a road is reached.

4 If you are in need of sustenance, the **Hare and Hounds** is 150 yards along the road to your left, but our way continues along the road to the right for a short distance to meet a signed footpath on

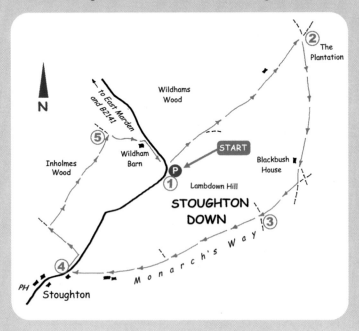

■ *The Monarch's Way near Stoughton* ■

the left. Follow the footpath uphill and at the edge of woodland turn right at a sign. Now remain on this lovely path for ¾ mile until it ends at a T-junction with a bridleway.

❺ Turn right downhill. Pass a house and continue along its drive to meet a road. Turn right along the road to soon re-join the car park and complete this enjoyable walk.

Place of interest nearby

The **Weald and Downland Open Air Museum** displays ancient buildings that have been rescued and carefully rebuilt in their original form. The museum is at Singleton, 4 miles east of Stoughton on the A286. ☎ 01243 811363.

2

West Itchenor and the Chichester Channel

■ *Walking alongside the Chichester Channel* ■

This wonderfully diverse walk begins by following the course of the Chichester Channel, a natural harbour popular with large flocks of wading birds. The tidal mud flats and saltings are designated as an Area of Outstanding Natural Beauty and a Site of Special Scientific Interest. This interesting level circuit is easy to follow and has many waterside picnic spots. After leaving the water's edge, the route passes the pretty thatched cottages of West Wittering before joining a delightful track leading to open fields with panoramic views from where the circuit makes its return.

Distance: 6 miles

Starting point: Pay and display car park in West Itchenor. GR SU798013

How to get there: West Itchenor is 4½ miles south-west of Chichester off the B2179. The car park is signed from the village street.

OS Map: Explorer 120 Chichester

Refreshments: There are plenty of picnic spots along the route, or visit the Old House at Home pub in West Wittering (tel. 01243 511234).

The Walk

❶ Go back to the village street and turn left passing the **Ship Inn** to reach the Chichester Channel. Turn left on a signed path directing you between a boatyard and **Jetty House**. At another boatyard, continue ahead on a tarmac path. When this turns right at a fork, go ahead and follow the water's edge.

❷ After rounding **Chalkdock Point**, the path passes a spit of land called **Horse Pond**. Here you should ignore a path to your left and go ahead on a boardwalk.

❸ At a scattered group of houses, follow the well-signed path between them to rejoin the water's edge. Later, 30 yards after passing a boathouse with a thatched cottage beyond, the way divides. Turn right through a gate and continue past a spit of land called **Ella Nore**. Ignore a path on your right.

4 After passing the rear of gardens, the way meets a large grassy area with sea views that is just perfect for a leisurely picnic. Here

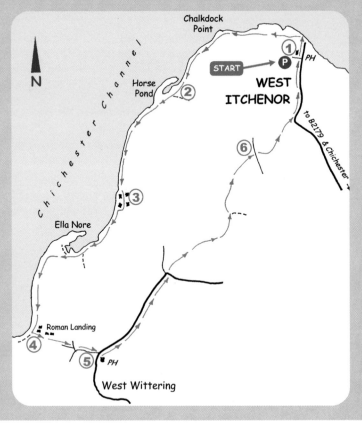

we leave the water by turning left at a gate which leads through the houses of **Roman Landing** on a signed footpath. After going between fields, continue on a narrow lane to meet a T-junction. Turn right for 30 yards before turning left along a road to reach the centre of **West Wittering** where the Old House at Home pub marks the halfway point of the circuit.

❺ Turn left along the main street signed to Chichester and remain alongside it for ½ mile. At a sharp right bend, leave the road and maintain direction along a farm track shared with cyclists. When the track bends sharp right, go diagonally left and follow a grassy path through fields to reach a drive.

■ *In West Wittering* ■

6 Cross the drive and continue on the path to finally reach the main street in **West Itchenor**. Turn left and follow the road past pretty houses to end the circuit back at the car park.

■ *A lovely field path near the end of the circuit* ■

Place of interest nearby

The remains of the spectacular **Fishbourne Roman Palace** include the largest collection of in-situ mosaics in Britain. The palace can be found 1 mile west of Chichester off the A259.
☎ 01243 789829.

③
Midhurst, the River Rother and Stedham

■ *The magnificent Stedham Mill House* ■

This delightfully diverse and enjoyable walk begins not far from the ruins of Cowdray House, an early Tudor mansion. Almost immediately, the route passes through rolling scenery before following a short residential road as it makes its way to the bank of the River Rother. After continuing through fields and peaceful woodland, the path rejoins the riverbank as it brings you to Stedham Mill. Although the mill has now gone, the miller's house remains. A quiet lane through the pretty village of Stedham leads to fields which are crossed before passing through woodland to rejoin the outward path.

Distance: 4¾ miles

Starting point: Cowdray House car park in North Street (A272) on the north-eastern edge of Midhurst.
GR SU887218

How to get there: Midhurst is 7 miles west of Petworth, on the A272.

OS Map: Explorer 133 Haslemere & Petersfield

Refreshments: There are plenty of places in North Street and the Half Moon pub is passed along the way (tel. 01730 818818).

The Walk

1 Go out to the **A272**, cross the road and turn right and then left into **Lambert's Lane**. At a sharp left bend bear right, pass a small parking area and continue between a house and a sports hall to reach a field. Go ahead along the left-hand field edge to reach a kissing gate on your left. Go through the gate and over a hillock, passing a paddock and a house, to meet a road.

2 Turn right along the road until it ends beside the **Half Moon pub** on the A272. Turn right over a small area of grass as directed by a sign for the long-distance **New Lipchis Way**. Soon after entering trees, follow the path right, and cross a stile. Continue ahead along the right-hand field edge and keep on to reach the bank of the **River Rother** and **Woolbeding Bridge**.

❸ Turn right over the bridge and continue along the road. At a right bend, fork left over a stile beside a National Trust sign and enter a field. Go ahead with a hedgerow on your right to reach the riverbank. Turn right over a stile beside a field gate and press on beside the river. As the path swings away from the river, turn right over a stile, enter woodland and climb a short rise. Turn left at the top and follow the well-defined path along the crest of the ridge in this beautiful bluebell wood.

❹ Soon after passing the barn of **Brambling Farm**, turn left at a marker post to re-join the riverbank. Turn right and follow the river. Turn left at a T-junction and cross a weir by **Stedham Mill**. Follow

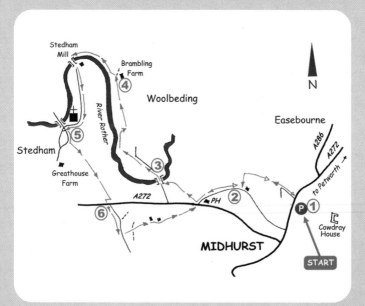

a tarmac drive past pretty cottages and through the graveyard of **St James's church** to meet a road junction.

■ *The route passes through delightful woodland* ■

⑤ Turn left. At a small triangle of grass bear left along a pretty lane. Look out for a signed path to your left where you pass a row of cottages to reach the polo training grounds of **Greathouse Farm**. Go diagonally half right towards an avenue of trees aiming 50 yards to the left of a tall clipped hedge. From the avenue, maintain direction and aim for a cut in a bank ahead of you. Pass down steps in the bank and follow the path over a stream and through woodland to reach the A272.

⑥ Cross the road, turn right and in 50 yards go left on a lane. Climb a rise ignoring a path on your left and at an open area in the forest, turn left on the **Serpent Trail**. Pass under power cables to reach a junction of paths in 20 yards. Ignore paths to left and right and continue ahead to reach a woodland track. Turn right along the track and when beside a house in the trees to your left, turn right on the signed path that now skirts the garden of a second house to meet a track. Follow this track, pass scattered houses and ignore a left fork to reach the A272 with the **Half Moon pub** opposite, from where you should retrace your outward steps to complete the circuit.

Place of interest nearby

Just a short walk east of the car park are the remains of **Cowdray House**, which was destroyed by fire in 1793. The ruin is highly evocative of Tudor times. ☎ 01730 810781.

4

Eartham Wood and a Roman road

■ *The well-preserved flint surface of Roman Stane Street* ■

This stunning walk begins by following a well-preserved section of Roman road that once linked Chichester to London. The route begins in majestic Eartham Wood, where the quiet walker has every chance of spotting wild deer among the beeches. Soon after meeting rolling downland at The Gumber, the way turns south and begins a gentle descent to lower ground before turning again for the home leg where it passes through a good variety of scenery with far-reaching views. Re-joining Eartham Wood, the route continues along a wide path through the woodland to complete this lovely walk.

Distance: 4½ miles

Starting point: Car park and picnic site in Eartham Wood. GR SU939106

How to get there: Eartham is signed off the A27 west of Fontwell. The car park is ¾ mile north of the village.

OS Map: Explorer 121 Arundel & Pulborough

Refreshments: The George Inn at Eartham, or picnic along the route.

The Walk

❶ From the car park, go back to the road and turn left as far as a vehicle barrier on the left. Turn left here on a gravel track. After 40 yards take the right-hand fork and remain on it for 1 mile to reach a large junction of tracks with a signpost.

*This track is **Stane Street**, a well-preserved Roman military road linking London to Chichester. The Roman name for it is unknown but the Saxons quite fittingly called it* Stone Street. *The Saxon word for* stone *is* stane *and modern mapmakers now use that version.*

❷ At the junction go ahead on the path signed to **Bignor**. After leaving woodland the way continues on the Roman road to meet rolling downland. Go ahead through a pedestrian gate and continue along the right side of a field. Pass through a gate at the far end of the field to meet another on your right in 30 yards.

3 Turn right here and continue to the buildings of **Gumber Farm** and **Bothy**. Pass through the farmyard and press on ahead along the farm drive. The drive bends right at **Warren Barn** but our route goes ahead on a forestry track through woodland. On leaving the wood, a path joins from the left. Here you should bear right and continue beside a field to meet a T-junction with a wide cart track.

4 Turn right along the cart track signed as a bridleway and when it forks at the edge of woodland, follow the left fork. As you exit the

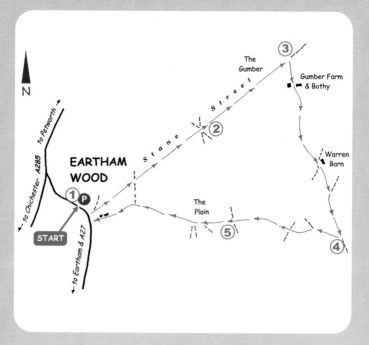

■ *The sheep-grazed pastures of Gumber Farm* ■

woodland, ignore a crossing path and continue ahead on the bridleway between fields to reach **Eartham Wood**.

5 Now press on ahead for 1 mile on this well-defined bridleway across **The Plain**, ignoring occasional side paths. As you leave the woodland, you pass a couple of forestry buildings and arrive at a road. Turn right along the road to reach the car park and the end of this super walk.

Place of interest nearby

Denmans Garden is a unique 20th-century garden beautifully planted for all-year interest. The plant centre stocks over 1,500 varieties of perennials and shrubs, some rare. It is off the A27 westbound, 1 mile west of Fontwell. ☎ 01243 542808.

⑤ Arundel, the River Arun and Burpham

■ *Arundel Castle is visible from much of the route* ■

This not-to-be-missed walk passes through stunning scenery and a splendid variety of wildlife habitats. After leaving Arundel, the way follows the bank of the River Arun through an increasingly tranquil landscape to meet the hamlet of Warningcamp. Here the scenery changes as the route continues through the dappled shade of woodland to meet a beautiful valley below Warningcamp Hill. Turning north, the circuit reaches its halfway point at the picturesque village of Burpham before descending its Saxon hill fort to rejoin the riverbank where panoramic views and an easy stroll back to Arundel await.

Distance: 5¾ miles

Starting point: Pay and display car park in Queen Street, Arundel. GR TQ021069

How to get there: Queen Street is off a roundabout on the A27, east of the town centre.

OS Map: Explorer 121 Arundel & Pulborough

Refreshments: The George and Dragon pub at the halfway point (tel. 01903 883131), or picnic along the route.

The Walk

❶ Leave the car park via a gate opposite the entrance and climb steps to the bank of the **Arun**. Turn right and follow the riverside path that offers great views of **Arundel castle**. The path eventually leads to a kissing gate with a railway line beyond.

❷ Cross the railway taking heed of the 'Stop Look Listen' sign and follow a quiet drive to meet a T-junction with a road. Turn left along the road and carry on to a left bend 140 yards after **Warningcamp House**. Turn right here, on a signed bridleway through woodland.

❸ At the end of woodland, go through a gate and continue on a well-trodden path along the valley floor below Warningcamp Hill. Remain in the valley as you pass three fingerposts. When woodland closes in on both sides, pass through a gate and go ahead on a cart track to meet a T-junction in 100 yards.

❹ Turn left, ignore a path forking left into woodland and follow a well-worn path uphill to meet a concrete farm drive. Turn left along the drive to meet a T-junction with a road in the hamlet of Wepham. Go right along the road for a few yards before turning left on a pretty lane. At a T-junction, go left to find the renowned **George and Dragon pub** in **Burpham** at the halfway point of the circuit.

❺ Turn left, pass the front of the pub and press on along the left side of a cricket pitch that sits on top of the Saxon hill fort. Pass a

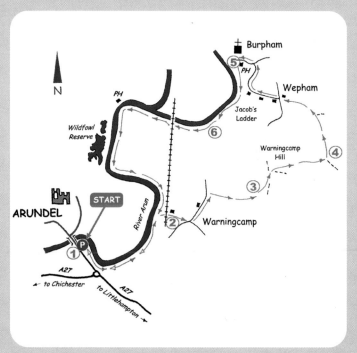

children's play area and continue on a fenced path where a glimpse through the hedgerow on your right confirms you are walking along the rim of the ancient fort. Go down the steps, now known as **Jacob's Ladder**, and at a right bend, cross a stile. Press on ahead along the right side of a field where the river is initially masked by reeds on your right.

6 Follow the riverside path over a series of stiles and re-cross the railway with caution. Keep to the riverbank where kestrels are often

■ *The path below Warningcamp Hill* ■

■ *The George and Dragon in Burpham* ■

seen hunting. The path leads you to a kissing gate where you rejoin your outward path, and make your return to **Arundel** to complete this great walk.

Place of interest nearby

The WWT **Arundel Wetland Centre** is adjacent to the River Arun and offers safaris on electric boats through its naturalised wetlands. Follow the tourist signs from Arundel.
☎ 01903 883355.

⑥ Amberley and the bank of the River Arun

■ *The view over Amberley* ■

This great little walk begins with a short, fairly steep hill that offers beautiful panoramic views over Amberley and beyond; it is the only hill on the route and, although steep should not trouble the average person. From these heights the way continues on a quiet downhill lane to meet the River Arun, a fine reward for your earlier exertion. There is an easy stroll alongside the river as it flows through tranquil scenery on its way to Amberley Wild Brooks. After leaving the riverbank the route crosses level fields and passes Amberley Castle where an easy stroll along one of the prettiest village streets in England brings the walk to a close.

Distance: 3 miles

Starting point: School Road, Amberley. GR TQ032130

How to get there: From the large roundabout on the A29 north of Arundel, take the B2139 to Amberley and after 2½ miles turn left into School Road. Park at the roadside.

OS Map: Explorer 121 Arundel & Pulborough

Refreshments: Amberley Village Tea Room (tel. 01798 839196).

The Walk

❶ Walk back along **School Road** to meet its junction with the B2139. Cross the road and continue along **Mill Lane** that soon rises quite sharply. Thankfully, the hill is short, so just take your time and soon you will reach a lane. Turn right along the lane and after passing an old quarry on your left (home to the Amberley Museum and Heritage Centre) re-join the B2139.

❷ Cross to the pavement opposite and turn left. Continue on the pavement and pass the entrances to the museum and Amberley station before going under a railway bridge. Turn right immediately after the bridge on a signed path that passes a small caravan park before bending left to meet the **River Arun**.

❸ Turn right along the riverbank and pass through tranquil scenery

■ *The tranquil River Arun* ■

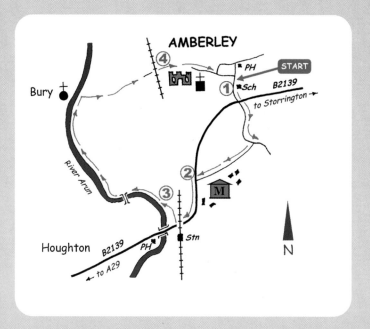

with lovely panoramic views. After 1 mile, turn right opposite the spire of **Bury church** on the far bank, on a signed path and cross three fields to meet a path bordered by hedgerows. Go ahead to the railway line and take note of the Stop Look Listen sign before crossing to the path opposite.

❹ Continue ahead on the path as it passes the side of **Amberley Castle** and joins a pretty village street which you should follow until it ends at **School Road**. Opposite is the **Amberley Village Tea Room** while a few yards to your right is the end of this good circuit.

■ *Amberley's streets are lined with pretty cottages* ■

Place of interest nearby

Amberley Museum and Heritage Centre is an open-air museum dedicated to the industrial heritage of the south-east. It is also home to a number of resident craftspeople who can be viewed as they use traditional methods in their work. Adjacent to Amberley railway station. ☎ 01798 831370.

West Chiltington and Nutbourne

■ *Church Street – the start of the walk* ■

This delightful short walk begins beside the 12th-century church of St Mary in the pretty village of West Chiltington. After passing through the churchyard, the way soon meets and crosses the fairways of a golf club to reach Gay Street from where an optional summertime excursion to Nutbourne Vineyard can be made. Continuing on, the route passes through the quiet hamlet of Nutbourne before crossing fields with panoramic views. The way then leads through a lovely wooded valley and passes a scenic lake before meeting rows of vines in Nyetimber Vineyard from where it makes its easy return.

Distance: 3 miles

Starting point: Church Street, West Chiltington.
GR TQ091183

How to get there: West Chiltington is on the Storrington
to Broadford Bridge road, 2½ miles north of Storrington.
Church Street is off the crossroads in the centre of the
village. Park at the roadside near the church.

OS Map: Explorer 121 Arundel & Pulborough

Refreshments: The Queen's Head pub in West
Chiltington (tel. 01798 812244) or the Rising Sun pub in
Nutbourne (tel. 01798 812191).

The Walk

1 Go through the kissing gate beside the village stocks and pass to
the right of **St Mary's church**. Turn right on a path outside the
churchyard and at a T-junction, turn right and continue to a road.
Go left along the road for 20 yards before turning right on a
bridleway between banks. At the end of the left-hand bank, turn left
on a bridleway to a golf course.

2 Watch out for flying golf balls as you go ahead across the fairways,
and at the far side maintain direction. Ignore a left fork under power
cables and follow a fenced path that ends at **Gay Street**.

A. *A short excursion to Nutbourne Vineyard from here will add ½ mile
to the route. Turn right along the road and in 200 yards go left*

*along the vineyard drive to the visitor centre. Open May to October
2 pm to 5 pm weekdays and 11 am to 5 pm weekends and bank
holidays.*

From point **A**, the route goes up the drive of **Stile Farm Cottage**
passing between the house and garage to meet a narrow path.
Continue along the right-hand side of two paddocks and pass the
end of a section of **Nutbourne Vineyard**. Go ahead at a gate and
press on between rows of vines on a track to meet a picturesque
cottage.

❸ Seek out a footpath by the right-hand wall of the cottage to skirt
the garden and pass a lake. At a field gate, go right over a stile,
cross a field to a stile opposite and follow a fenced path to the
village of **Nutbourne**. Turn right along the village street and pass

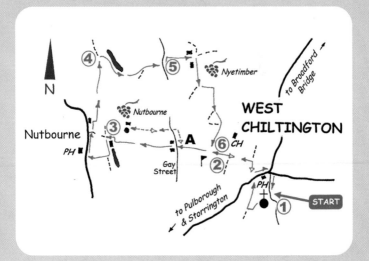

the **Rising Sun pub**. Turn right at a road junction, and in 40 yards go left on a well-trodden footpath. At a building, turn right over a stile and press on along the left side of a field. Maintain direction over a second field and continue ahead.

4. Look out for a signed path on your right which leads downhill and passes the end of a scenic lake. Cross a footbridge and continue uphill through woodland. At the end of an equestrian centre on your right, continue through a gate and in 10 yards bear right through a garden to meet a drive to re-join **Gay Street**.

5. Climb steps opposite and turn left beside the vines of **Nyetimber**

■ *This idyllic lake is passed along the way* ■

Vineyard. Turn right along the end of the rows and go ahead on a drive to pass the vineyard offices. Follow the drive rightwards to meet a junction of tracks. Turn left and in 90 yards follow the narrowing path rightwards between banks to re-join the golf course. Ignore a bridleway forking right and continue ahead along an avenue of trees to meet a T-junction and your outward path.

6 Turn left, re-cross the fairways and seek out a bridleway in the tree line opposite. Go ahead on the path walked earlier and turn right at a T-junction to meet a road. Turn left along the road to pass the **Queen's Head pub** before turning right into **Church Street** to end this enjoyable circuit.

Place of interest nearby

Nutbourne Vineyard. Learn how grapes are grown and taste the award-winning wines. See above for opening times. Gay Street, Nutbourne. ☎ 01798 815196.

Horsham and St Leonard's Forest

■ *A boarded walk through the woodland* ■

This glorious woodland circuit begins within a mile of Horsham town centre and is surprisingly peaceful and delightfully rural. The route passes through Leechpool Wood to join a section of the 90-mile High Weald Landscape Trail from Horsham to Rye. The easily followed route leads you through the peace and tranquillity of St Leonard's Forest where wide tracks make the perfect picnic spot. After leaving the forest and the long-distance path, the way passes through a variety of pretty landscapes before later rejoining the outward path to make its return.

Distance: 5 miles

Starting point: Car park at Leechpool and Owlbeech Woods. GR TQ194313

How to get there: The well-signed car park is off Harwood Road (B2195) on the eastern perimeter of Horsham.

OS Map: Explorer 124 Crawley & Horsham

Refreshments: The Norfolk Arms pub is a short distance north on the B2195 (tel. 01403 750676) or picnic along the route.

The Walk

1 From the car park entrance, turn left beside the road and in 25 yards turn left again on a signed footpath. The path leads through a wood and brings you to a small bridge over a brook. Cross the bridge and follow the path rightwards. This later becomes boarded before meeting a drive and the **High Weald Landscape Trail**. Turn left and follow the drive.

2 When the drive bends left at the gate of **St Leonard's Park House**, fork right to a field gate. Here turn left on a signed path alongside a field. At the field's end continue ahead on the well-trodden path. Cross a drive and go ahead on an indistinct path to the right of a cart track that crosses an open area. At the end of the open area, follow a narrower path downhill beside a field.

3 As you enter woodland ignore a path on your right and go ahead on a cart track. At a right bend, fork left on the narrower **High Weald Landscape Trail**. After going over one crossing track, a second and much larger track is reached at the top of a rise.

This track is known as Mick Mill's Race and has many stories regarding its name; from a Michael Mills who planted an avenue of trees here in 1720, to a local man of that name who is said to have raced the Devil along the track – I favour the former!

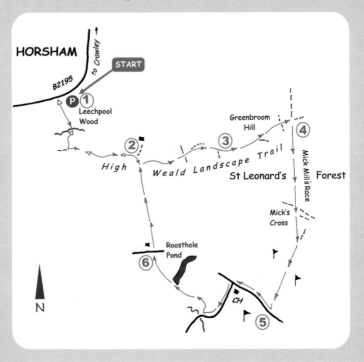

④ Turn right along this wonderful track to meet a junction of tracks known as **Mick's Cross** in ½ mile. Leave the long-distance path by continuing straight ahead. In 80 yards ignore a bridleway on your left. Keep ahead through woodland to meet a T-junction. Turn right here along a bridleway that passes between the fairways of **Mannings Heath Golf Club** before finally ending at a road.

⑤ Turn right along the road and 50 yards after passing the golf club entrance, turn left on a lane. At a left bend in a dip, go right over a stile beside a stream. Climb a small open hillock and continue to another stile at the woodland edge. Follow the well-trodden path along the edge of woodland and pass the end of **Roosthole Pond**.

■ *In St Leonard's Forest* ■

■ *The peaceful track in the forest known as Mick Mill's Race* ■

6 Later cross a road and go ahead along a farm track to reach a field gate in ½ mile with **St Leonard's Park House** beyond. Now retrace your steps back along the drive remembering to turn right along the boarded path through woodland.

Place of interest nearby

Horsham Museum is housed in a medieval building in one of the most picturesque streets in Sussex and contains displays covering hundreds of years of local history. It can be found at the Causeway, off the A281 in the centre of Horsham. ☎ 01403 254959.

Cowfold and Crabtree

■ *The route follows scenic field paths* ■

This lovely field ramble crosses peaceful scenic farmland between the village of Cowfold and its smaller northern neighbour Crabtree that nestles below the High Weald. The route passes through a rural idyll brimming with wild flowers, fruit-bearing hedgerows and wildlife – a combination that makes one of the best pastoral scenes in Sussex. Leaving Cowfold on well-signed paths, the way heads north through gently undulating countryside to reach its turning point on the outskirts of Crabtree. Turning south, the route continues through attractive fields as it makes an easy return to Cowfold.

Distance: 4½ miles

Starting point: The car park by Cowfold recreation ground. GR TQ215225

How to get there: Cowfold is at the crossroads of the A272 and A281, 3 miles west of Bolney. The car park is off the A272 at the centre of the village.

OS Map: Explorer 134 Crawley & Horsham

Refreshments: The Coach House pub just north of the crossroads (tel. 01403 864247).

The Walk

1 From the car park entrance, turn right along a lane named **Fairfield Cottages** and turn right on a signed footpath alongside the recreation ground. Cross a stile on your left and continue on the well-used path. At the end of a garden turn left. After passing along a field edge, go ahead through a tree line and cross a field aiming to the right of a house. Pass through a gate and cross a bridge to meet a junction of paths.

2 Turn left, pass under power cables to meet a field and follow its edge as it swings right. In 150 yards fork left on a signed path that remains parallel to the field. Pass the buildings of **Pict's Farm** and cross a stile ahead of you. Follow the right side of a paddock and continue on the signed path to reach a lane. Turn left along the lane and after going downhill, turn right on a track leading to **Graffields**. Cross a cattle grid.

❸ Follow the track and 80 yards after passing the house, fork left over a grassy area to meet a track to the right of a second house. Pass through a gate and now follow the track between fields. After

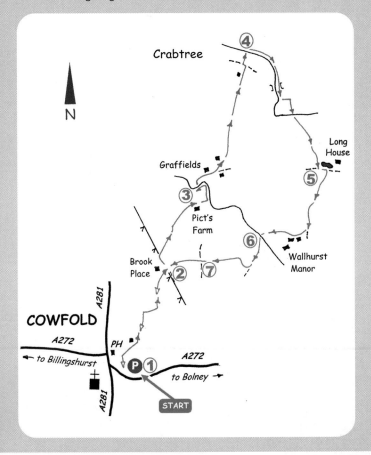

passing a house, ignore paths to left and right and remain on the track to reach a country lane.

4 Turn right along the lane that soon becomes unmade and pass a couple of cottages. Immediately after crossing a bridge, turn left on a signed footpath. At a marker post go right over a stile and follow the left field edge to rejoin the track. Go diagonally left to a stile, enter a field and follow an indistinct grassy path diagonally half left. At the far side continue on a well-trodden path to meet and cross a second field.

5 At the top of a rise turn left by a marker post. Turn right at a second marker post by a garden pond and continue alongside woodland. Pass through a gate and follow the well-defined path through the trees. At a field continue ahead along its left edge and cross a stile at its end. The path now divides. Fork right on the narrower path that passes the rear of houses and ends at a country lane.

6 Go left along the lane for 25 yards before turning right into a field. Go ahead beside a fence and in 120 yards cross a stile on your right. Now turn diagonally left towards the right side of a prominent oak tree. Ignore a stile by a direction post and turn right alongside the field. As the field edge swings right, go left on a signed path and follow a cart track alongside a field.

7 When the cart track turns right, keep ahead, ignoring paths to left and right. Soon ignore a stile on your right but, 35 yards later, fork right over a second stile and continue through trees to rejoin your outward path by the footbridge. Cross the bridge and retrace your earlier steps by going diagonally left over a field and following the well-signed footpath back to **Cowfold** to complete this lovely ramble.

■ *A shady path under a spreading oak* ■

Place of interest nearby

St Peter's church, at the centre of Cowfold, dates from the 13th century although much of what exists today originates from Henry VIII's time. The great Victorian stained-glass artist C. E. Kempe had a hand in some of the modern windows.

⑩ Woods Mill and the River Adur

■ *The River Adur* ■

This pleasurable and scenic route begins at Woods Mill, one of Sussex Wildlife Trust's nature reserves, before following a stream through level fields with panoramic views to the South Downs. A short section of the Downs Link long-distance path brings you to the River Adur where the route turns and follows the river as it meanders through the wonderfully expansive scenery of the Low Weald. After leaving the riverbank, the way continues along level paths and tracks before rejoining the Downs Link where a leisurely stroll brings you back to your outward path.

Distance: 5½ miles

Starting point: The car park at Woods Mill.
GR TQ218138

How to get there: Go south from Henfield on the A2037 and after 1¼ miles turn left into Horn Lane to meet the car park in 20 yards.

OS Map: Explorer 122 Brighton & Hove

Refreshments: Plenty of picnic spots on the route or eateries in Henfield.

The Walk

❶ From the car park, walk back to the **A2037** and turn left along this unavoidable stretch of road for 200 yards. At a right bend, turn right through a kissing gate and go ahead along a grassy cart track with a stream to your left. When the cart track ends at a field gate, cross a stile beside it, ignore a path to your right and remain alongside the stream, later ignoring a path on the left.

❷ At the end of the field, cross a stile to reach the **Downs Link** long-distance path. Remember this junction because it is from here that we make our return.

The path is along the track bed of a railway that suffered one of Dr Beeching's cuts during the 1960s. Beginning on the outskirts of Guildford in Surrey, it ends 37 miles later at Shoreham.

Turn left along the track to meet an old railway bridge over the **River Adur**. Cross the bridge and turn immediately right on a signed bridleway which follows the riverbank through peaceful fields.

❸ After 1 mile turn right over a bridge and follow a bridleway that passes the buildings of **New Inn Farm** to meet a drive. Continue ahead along the drive and remain on this bridleway as it makes use of a variety of drives, tracks and paths for ¾ mile.

❹ When the bridleway finally ends at a road, continue ahead and pass an industrial building. Opposite a couple of houses, turn right on the signed **Downs Link** and remain on it for ¾ mile until your

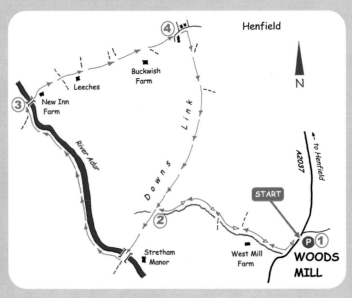

■ *Wild flowers lining the way* ■

outward path is met on the left. Now retrace your steps alongside the stream until you reach the **A2037** where a left turn brings you back to the car park and the end of this good circuit.

Place of interest nearby

Henfield Museum exhibits range from fossils and flint implements, to farm tools and household items from the Tudor, Georgian and Victorian periods. The museum can be found at Coopers Way, High Street, Henfield. ☎ 01273 492507.

11

The Clayton Windmills and Ditchling Beacon

■ *On the way to North Bottom* ■

With panoramic views along its entire length, this route must rate as one of the most scenic walks in the south-east. After leaving the windmills, known as Jack and Jill, the circuit heads across undulating downland to reach its most southerly point at Lower Standean from where it turns and passes through the glories of North Bottom, one of three beautiful elongated folds in the south flank of the Downs where the air is sweet and the views expansive. With a steady climb that should not trouble the average person, the way heads for Ditchling Beacon and the popular South Downs Way. This long-distance path offers stunning panoramic views and easy walking as the route returns to the end of this great circuit.

Distance: 4½ miles

Starting point: The car park by the Clayton windmills.
GR TQ303134

How to get there: The windmills are signed off the A273,
just south of Clayton which is 1 mile south of Hassocks.

OS Map: Explorer 122 Brighton & Hove

Refreshments: The Jack and Jill pub in Clayton
(tel. 01273 843595) or picnic along the way.

The Walk

❶ From the car park entrance, go left on a stony track and pass the
Jack and Jill windmills. At a fork, bear right on the **South Downs
Way** to pass the buildings of **New Barn Farm**. Press on ahead at
a crossing track and maintain direction alongside a golf club. After
climbing a rise a T-junction is met.

❷ Turn left here on a bridleway to meet a tree-line and then go right
through a gate where the bridleway continues alongside a field.
Go left through a second gate and continue along the right-hand
edge of a field. Ignore a gate on your right at the brow of a rise
and continue along the field edge. Follow the field edge leftwards
to meet a gate. Turn right through the gate and continue on a
downhill cart track passing a brick barn.

❸ Fork left 60 yards before the farm buildings at **Lower Standean**.
After 40 yards pass through a gate and continue along the right

side of a rising field. Go through a second gate and follow an indistinct cart track that swings right then left to meet the foot of **North Bottom**, a dull name for such a beautiful place.

4 Press on up the valley floor and pass through a gate on your right to enter a field. Continue along the left edge of this field and go through a gate at its far end. Continue up the valley floor on an indistinct path that soon begins to climb more steeply between fields. Take your time and admire the views behind you as you climb towards **Ditchling Beacon**. After the path flattens you arrive at a T-junction with the **South Downs Way**.

5 **Ditchling Beacon** is a few yards to your right while our way is left along the long-distance path that after 1½ miles of easy panoramic walking returns you to the windmills and the end of this great circuit.

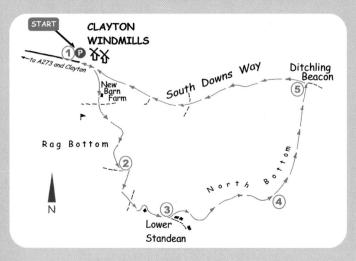

■ *Admiring the view from Ditchling Beacon* ■

Place of interest nearby

Ditchling Museum. Ditchling's recognition during the early 20th century as a centre for print, calligraphy, weaving and other crafts is reflected in a permanent collection in the museum in Church Lane. Various exhibitions and events are held throughout the year. ☎ 01273 844744.

12

Ardingly Reservoir and the Ouse Valley

■ *The start of the walk* ■

This stunning walk is jam packed full of beautiful scenery ranging from waterside views over the reservoir, tranquil woodland, scenic farm tracks and field paths. The outward route follows the High Weald Landscape Trail which, after passing through majestic woodland, turns west and continues through the grounds of Borde Hill. Fine field paths with extensive views lead to the hamlet of Brook Street before the route turns again and joins the Sussex Ouse Valley Way where it continues along lovely farm tracks and under Balcombe's famous railway viaduct before following pretty field paths beside the infant River Ouse to complete the circuit.

Distance: 6½ miles

Starting point: The car park at Ardingly Reservoir (pay on entry). GR TQ335286

How to get there: Ardingly is 6 miles south-west of East Grinstead on the B2028. From Ardingly, follow College Road south-west for 1 mile before turning right along the drive to the reservoir.

OS Map: Explorer 134 Crawley & Horsham and Explorer 135 Ashdown Forest

Refreshments: Picnic along the route or at the reservoir picnic area.

The Walk

❶ From the car park, climb a slope to the water's edge by a sailing club. Continue up a slope to the left of the building to a directional post and turn left on the **High Weald Landscape Trail**. Follow this well-signed path through fields and across a bridge over a stream. Press on to reach woodland and continue on the well-trodden path to cross the railway and meet the buildings of **River's Farm**.

❷ Go ahead along a farm track before crossing a stile and continuing through two fields following the signs. Pass the side of a house to meet **Copyhold Lane**. Turn right and follow the lane to a T-junction. Here, go left for 200 yards before turning right on a bridleway that enters the grounds of **Borde Hill**.

3 Go ahead, pass a car park and continue through a field gate. Follow the bridleway as it passes a ha-ha from which there are views of the house and gardens but, as a non-paying guest, you must not wander from this path. When the track ends at a drive, go ahead through a gate and cross a field. Stay on top of the ridge to enjoy a panoramic view of the Weald. The path is well-signed and will lead you through fields and woodland to reach the hamlet of **Brook Street**.

4 Turn right along the B2036 and after 50 yards go left into **Spark's Lane**. Pass the entrance to **Lower Spark's Farm** and go ahead on the bridleway where you soon leave the landscape trail. At the end of woodland on your right, turn right and continue along the field edge beside the trees. Pass through a tree line and go

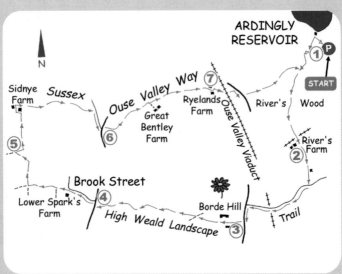

diagonally left across the next field to meet a track by a gate and signpost to join the **Sussex Ouse Valley Way**.

5 Turn right along the track to meet **Sidnye Farm**. Go left in front of barns and then turn right alongside them towards the farmhouse. Now turn right and continue on the farm drive until it ends at a lane where a right turn soon brings you to a road.

■ *The impressive Balcombe Ouse Valley Viaduct* ■

6 Turn left and in 20 yards go right, along the drive to **Great Bentley Farm**. When the drive swings right to meet the house, turn left through a gate and follow a path along the right side of a field. When the field edge bends rightwards keep ahead, cross a stream and then turn diagonally right over a field to cross a stile in the hedgerow. Maintain direction over the next field, cross a stile and go ahead to meet **Ryelands Farm**.

7 Pass the buildings and in 30 yards cross a stile on your right. Continue on a path that leads under the stunning **Balcombe Ouse Valley Viaduct** to reach a road. Turn right along the road, cross a small bridge and 15 yards later turn left on a public footpath that follows the course of the infant **River Ouse**. The path leads to the bridge you crossed earlier and from here you should turn left and re-trace your steps to complete this great circuit.

Place of interest nearby

The Royal Botanic Gardens at Wakehurst Place contain over 450 acres of country estate, ornamental gardens and temperate woodland. Off the B2028 1 mile north of Ardingly. ☎ 01444 894066.